THE GREEKS

THE GREEKS

Edited and Translated by Kimon Friar
Photography by John Veltri

With a Preface by **Lawrence Durrell** and
Commentary by **Odysseus Elytis**

Doubleday & Company, Inc.
Garden City, New York
1984

Library of Congress Catalog Card Number 83-40282
ISBN 0-385-19067-0

Acknowledgment
Some of the translations used in this book were originally published in *Modern Greek Poetry*, Simon and Schuster, copyright © 1973 by Kimon Friar, and *The Sovereign Sun*, Temple University Press, 1974. The publisher and book producer wish to thank Simon and Schuster and Temple University Press for permission to reprint some of the poems.

All translation and notes in *The Greeks* are by Kimon Friar, Athens, Greece.

Preface copyright © 1984 by Lawrence Durrell

Printed in Italy by New Interlitho S.p.A. - Milan

DEDICATION

To the memory of ANDREAS CARIOLOU, Cypriot sponge diver, underwater explorer and teacher whose freedom loving spirit touched many lives, and who taught me to dive into the depth of the Greek Soul.

My gratitude goes out to the Greek people everywhere for opening their hearts with great hospitality and making this book possible.

JOHN VELTRI

Preface

With these photos John Veltri has made a striking contribution to our knowledge and feelings about modern Greece, for he uses his mind as his camera and the eloquence of his vision lies in its gravity, in its deliberate refusal of a glib prolixity—for Greece can offer that side too, as any travel poster will show you. The light is so rich and the beauty so profuse that almost anywhere you direct your lens will yield something dramatic, colorful, profuse; in consequence to capture the austere reality of the place, its stark refusal to be anything but its own naked self, one has to learn what to eliminate. Happily we can see the difference when we look at the ordinary travel folder. It is not inaccurate as to detail; it is simply not truthful enough for a poet who feels the tragic life and death struggle of nature which underlies the superficially beautiful harbors, churches, ikons. They have made a cliché of Greece as they have of Tahiti, Italy, Spain. For someone with a sense of place, of a culture, of a national identity, it is necessary to get beyond the Club Méditerrané mentality. And in John Veltri Greece has found an interpreter of great elegance and fastidiousness, keeping strictly to the truth as his mind discerns it. This results in a series of beautifully simple and coherent visions of the eternal Greek temperament both modern and ancient—indeed there is no difference between them when once one feels the pulse-beat of the place. Every pinch of Greek dust contains the unfolded calyx of the created vase, every smile on a child's face is a secret rainbow full of promise. This book is a loving anthology of the Greek vision put together by poets specially for the poet in everyman. "Fair Greece! Proud Relic!" wrote Shelley. He would have sensed the pride and the indomitable courage of the Hellenes in these magnificent, tender and thoughtful pictures. We are grateful to be reminded by John Veltri of the fierce and rich core of the Hellenic experience which is still ours to enjoy and appraise through these fine camera poems.

LAWRENCE DURRELL

The Retina of John Veltri

When an artist says "I see," he really means "I make others see."

Many have passed through Greece, but if a modern, mythological Sphinx were to ask them, as they were leaving, "What have you seen?", I am afraid that most of them would lose in playing this deadly game. A long tradition, that began with the renaissance, has continued to nourish the nostalgic traveler into the ancient past with a series of ready-made and overly beautiful images even before he comes to Greece. It so happens, unfortunately, that these impose themselves on the memory and endure longer on the eye's retina than the true image of real objects, often to such an extent that even the past itself is rendered lethal.

Nevertheless, it is also true that there is no country so inextricably bound up with its past. Yet even though Greece may not itself seek to do so, it transforms its past into a continuous present. In such a way, indeed, that for a hunter of images, such as a photographer, it becomes difficult to find a "parallel" amid all these transformations and, what is still more difficult, to find the ultimate "one" which emerges from the diverse moments of a unique reality. In other words, the photographer must work exactly like a poet. It is this, I believe, that John Veltri has succeeded in doing, a great accomplishment.

Greece bewilders the visitor and causes him to lose his way. It is, at one and the same time, very small and very large in space and time. In an area of only a few thousand square kilometers there is room for a hundred and more high mountains, a thousand and more islands, big and small. But on the other hand it contains many thousand kilometers of history where the activities of cultural groups are so repeated with the same good or bad characteristics that ultimately they may be summarized into four or five particular types. Yet with all these differences, they are bound together by one language, for there exist even today people who speak the same tongue from ancient into modern times, a unique phenomenon in the Western world. And everywhere there exist the same natural elements—rocks, trees, seas—inflamed by the same sun, inhabited by the same supernatural powers.

Even though Veltri decided to divide his material according to the four natural elements—and from the point of view of his book's economy he did well to do so—his careful evaluation of the documents he offers us permits us to ascertain that, consciously or unconsciously, he has interwoven the physiognomy of Greece with those same three components which, with their sequences and correspondences, constitute the invisible yet all-inclusive continuity of Greece in its second but true being: I mean, the light, the sea, and poverty.

Of course it seems a kind of inverted arrogance to praise poverty. Nevertheless, throughout the centuries, poverty, together with the sufferings that follow in its wake, has come to take on in Greece another, an ethical meaning, and to develop its own specific gravity. This was a virtue we watched as it took on the form and features of the warrior among men and of endurance among women, and which ultimately made possible the obstinate survival of a people during persistent waves of conquerors. The writhing shapes of solitary trees, the titanic statures of rocks, the emaciated bodies of Orthodox saints, and the furrowed but always proud faces of the peasants show in full range what I want to say, and which Veltri has sensed both with the discernment of a historian and the observation of a psychologist.

The sea, on the other hand, fought poverty in a completely unexpected manner. For the sea, in Greece, is another story altogether. It has no relationship to the endless flowing valley which opens up before other coastal countries. It is a familiar and friendly element, a tranquil tongue which penetrates into and cuts up the land in a thousand ways, a second terrain which may in its own way be sown and give of its harvest to men. It has been endowed with godlike qualities. The sea follows one everywhere. If you find yourself high up on some mountain you know that at any moment, wherever it may be, on a certain turn, you will come upon it, inviting and irreproachable. If you sail upon it, you feel it will do you no harm, no matter how tempestuous it may be; besides, wherever you may turn your head you will discern far on the horizon the ridge of another shore, the curve of an island reposing upon it with infinite grace. One can repeat to some purpose what has so often been said: This element which elsewhere separates men here unites them. Under the keels of the caiques, trained to plow the Aegean ceaselessly, from the Peninsula to Anatolia, a mythical world of fishes, sponges, old shipwrecks and half-sunken cities give to the Odysseus of every period, together with the sense of adventure innate in every man, the allure of the unknown, the anticipation of wonders. Even the profits of commerce come close to the enchantment of legend. This is one more characteristic of the Greek which he retains on his face scorched by brine—and this Veltri has captured with an instantaneous movement—the traces of that hero who at one and the same time fights for some sort of daily bread and for some sort of freedom, without forgetting that the latter is very often, for him, more indispensable than the first.

But here we have reached another mystery, the third of those threads which earlier I said weave the destiny of this region. At one extreme it touches that which we name *history* (and which, up to a certain point, it can explain), and at the other extreme touches that which we name *the surpassing truth* belonging to the realm of the spirit. One may speak of light from a technical point of view, but this is not what I should like to sanction among Veltri's assets, since others of his colleagues have wielded it with more or less the same success. Instead I should like to speak of light in its mystic function, of the despotic presence of the sun and its invisible machine, which may be discerned also under the surface of contemporary as well as of ancient tragedy. Poets from other lands who have never set foot in Greece, such as Holderlin, and great Greek poets such as Solomós, Sikelianós and Seféris, have given it, or have tried to present it, each in his own manner, or as much as one can "present" something which is, of its very nature, elusive. Similarly Veltri has tried, by means of the lens, to present us with that something, as much as he can. That is, by means of the image. And not even with the image. With a fugitive moment of the image: a luster in the glance of a child, a translucency in the shallow waters of a seashore, a white hair isolated in the mustache of an old man. In this reading of another kind, it is necessary, of course, for the spectator also to participate. If out of the total a certain "knowledge" emerges, this is the "action of the true spectator" which succeeds behind the simple forms of a country and its people in deciphering and recomposing its history and its psychology.

Beyond any kind of eloquence, John Veltri has stood face to face with the sometimes divine shapes of its islands. With the lean bodies of its boys. With its landscapes so filled with desolation and mystery. With its ancient statues, there where time stopped them, their hands outstretched as though to capture or to shake off an inexplicable destiny, the blanks of their eyes shoring up the infinite.

ODYSSEUS ELÝTIS
Athens
Translated by KIMON FRIAR

Photographer's Preface

Greece is a country of extremes, of contrasts bold and subtle. To even scratch the surface of a country as complex as Greece, you must spend much time traveling, building up a composite image of mountain ranges, hazardous roads, fertile plains, winter snow, burning sun and glittering summer surf. To know it intimately is to know more than languid, hot summer afternoons and the calm, clear waters of resort locations where tourists congregate. To see more than the picture-postcard surface is to experience Greece at different times of the year, to feel its year-round hardships as well as its joys, to know the turbulent sea and damp, cool mornings when life huddles around a fire and friendships are less gregarious and more intense.

I was fortunate to go to Greece first not as a tourist but as a working photographer on assignment to cover an underwater archaeological excavation of an ancient Greek ship, which had sunk in the third century B.C. off the coast of Cyprus. My experience with Greeks in Cyprus whetted my thirst for a deeper understanding of the Greeks and of Greece itself, which after more than fourteen years has culminated in this book.

THE EARTH is rugged and harsh. As George Seféris, one of the poets represented, expresses it: "Our country is enclosed, all mountains whose roof is low sky night and day." These mountains have divided Greece historically, making inevitable the development of isolated traditions. This chapter includes some of the major architectural relics of ancient Greek civilization, unearthed yet everywhere returning again to the earth, the weight of the past carried into the present.

THE WATER is a major means of communication between the islands and mainland, between villages that live on and by the sea. This section pictures the attitudes and life that have historically emerged from the seas: fishing, sponge-diving and the modern accretions, underwater archaeology.

FIRE. The people of rural Greece are the subject in this section. The villagers, farmers and shepherds whose lives are on the soil and whose roots are still firmly fixed in tradition are the soul of Greece.

AIR. In this section the contrasts and ironies are shown, the mixtures and currents that are changing Greece. And the return, always the return, the pull of the past despite modernization, the influx of foreign industry and tourism.

In putting together this book of photographs and poetry I have tried to select images that are most typical of a particular location and also images and attitudes that are representative of all of Greece. I have also sought the unusual, those aspects that are hidden from the casual tourist, for Greece is in many ways a mysterious country, inaccessible to immediate comprehension and full of contradictions.

I have meant this book to be a collage of images, attitudes and impressions from which readers can draw their own conclusions. A final felicitous touch is supplied by the garland of Greek poems supplied by my friend Kimon Friar the poet translator to whom we owe so much. His work in the field of Greek letters is too well known for me to do more than salute it in passing; but these fine scrupulous translations bring a breath of finality and authenticity to the book as a whole.

Here then is Greece, from the Greeks: "The world has no handles, for one man to walk off with it over his shoulder."

JOHN VELTRI

13

Uprooted tree: The Republic of Cyprus

EARTH

from GYMNOPAEDIA

Give me your hands, give me your hands, give me your hands.

I saw in the night
the pointed peak of the mountain
I saw the field in the distance flooded
with the light of the unapparent moon
I saw, turning my head
the black stones clustered
and my life stretched like a chord
beginning and end
the last moment;
my hands.

He sinks who carries the huge stone;
these stones I carried as long as I could
these stones I loved as long as I could
these stones, my destiny.
Wounded by my own earth
tormented by my own shirt
condemned by my own gods,
these stones.

. . . .

Voice out of stone out of sleep
deeper here where the world darkens,
memory of toil rooted in a rhythm
that beat on the earth with feet
forgotten.
Bodies sunken in the foundations of the other time, naked. Eyes
riveted, riveted on the spot
which you cannot discern however you try;
the soul
that struggles to become your soul.

Even the silence is no longer yours
here where the millstones stopped.

GEORGE SEFÉRIS

16

Ancient fortress of Mycenae, Northern Peloponnesus

Fortress wall of Mycenae

Fallen columns of an ancient temple at Olympia

from MYTH OF OUR HISTORY

XXII

Because so very much has passed before our eyes
that even our eyes saw nothing, but far beyond
and behind us memory like a white cloth one night in a walled place

on which we saw strange visions, stranger than you,
drift and vanish into the motionless foliage of a pepper tree;

because we knew this fate of ours so well
wandering amid broken stones, three or six thousand years
searching amid ruined buildings that could have been, perhaps, our homes
trying to remember dates and heroic deeds;
shall we be able to?

because we were bound and scattered
and fought, as they said, with imaginary difficulties
lost, then finding again a road full of blind battalions
sinking in marshes and in the Lake of Marathon,
shall we be able to die in a normal way?

GEORGE SEFÉRIS

Stone corridor of the ancient fortress of Tiryns, Northern Peloponnesus

Standing column at ancient Olympia

Colonnade of the ancient Athenian Acropolis

Propylaea, main entrance to the Athenian Acropolis

from KING OF ASINE

And the poet looks at the stones and lingers, asking himself
are there I wonder
among these broken lines peaks edges hollows and curves
are there I wonder
here at the meeting place of wind rain and ruin
are there the movement of feature the form of the affection
of those who have so strangely dwindled in our lives
of those who have remained wave-shadows and thoughts boundless as the sea
or no, perhaps nothing remains but the weight only
nostalgia for the weight of a living existence.

GEORGE SEFÉRIS

Standing remains of a rotunda at the ancient holy site of Delphi

from KING OF ASINE

IV
The Argonauts
And if the soul
is ever to know itself
it must gaze
into the soul:
the stranger and the enemy, we have seen him in the mirror.

GEORGE SEFÉRIS

Eroded by wind and surf, timeless form emerges on the coast of Cyprus

from KING OF ASINE

XXI

We who set out on this pilgrimage
have looked on broken statues
forgot ourselves and said that life cannot so easily be lost
that death has its uncharted roads
and a justice of its own;

that when we die upright on our feet,
made one in the brotherhood of stone
united in hardness and weakness,
the ancient dead escape the circle and are resurrected
and smile in a strange stillness.

GEORGE SEFÉRIS

Bronze Charioteer, Delphi Museum

ANCIENT AMPHITHEATER

When toward noon the Greek youth found himself in the center
of an ancient amphitheater, and yet as handsome as They had been,
he let out a shout (not of astonishment, for astonishment
he felt not at all and, even if he had,
would certainly not have shown it), a simple shout,
perhaps out of the untamed joy of his youth
or simply to try out the acoustics of the place. Opposite,
from the precipitous mountain, the echo answered—
the Greek echo, which does not imitate or repeat
but simply continues to a height immeasurable
the eternal cry of the dithyramb.

YÁNNIS RÍTSOS

Ancient amphitheater at Epidaurus

from DE RERUM NATURA

What would the earth have been without us?
Anonymous, insubstantial, desolate.

What would the sky have been without us?

Shapes without light and without one voice
To name them, without perpetuity.

And what sort of thing would God have been?
A thing without name and without splendor.
What flesh would he have taken to manifest himself
Without flesh on earth, what face
Without the human face,
Without human shape or clothing,
What blows and blood, what suffering
Without human suffering:
Behold the man, behold God.
Without human death, without
Burial and lamentation, without resurrection.

What would Death have been without us?

GEORGE THÉMELIS

Monastery buildings at Meteora

Village church, Yerolimin

from MYTH OF OUR HISTORY

XVII

Astyanax

Now that you are going take with you the child
who first saw light under that plane tree,
on a day when trumpets resounded and weapons gleamed
and sweating horses bent down to touch
the green surface of water in the trough
with their moist nostrils.

The olive trees with the wrinkles of our fathers
the rocks with the knowledge of our fathers
and the blood of our brother alive on the earth
were a hardy joy a rich order
for souls who understood their prayer.

Now that you are going, now that the day of reckoning
dawns, now when nobody knows
whom he shall kill and how he shall end,
take with you the child who first saw light
under the leaves of that plane tree
and teach him to meditate on trees.

GEORGE SEFÉRIS

Ancient olive tree, Republic of Cyprus

from HEROIC AND ELEGIAC SONG
FOR THE LOST LIEUTENANT
OF THE ALBANIAN CAMPAIGN

XIV

Now the dream in the blood throbs more swiftly
The truest moment of the world rings out:
Liberty,
Greeks show the way in the darkness:
L I B E R T Y
For you the eyes of the sun shall fill with tears of joy.

Rainbow-beaten shores fall into the water
Ships with open sails voyage on the meadows
The most innocent girls
Run naked in men's eyes
And modesty shouts from behind the hedge
Boys! there is no other earth more beautiful

The truest moment of the world rings out!

ODYSSEUS ELÝTIS

Eroded sandstone, north coast of Cyprus

WATER

Churches and vaulted houses of Thera (Santorini)

Church steeple on the Island of Thira (Santorini)

from AXION ESTI

GENESIS III
    But before hearing wind or music
    as I set out to find a clearing
(ascending an endless red tract of sand
and erasing History with my heel)
    I struggled with my bedsheets What I was looking for
    was as innocent and tremulous as a vineyard
    as deep and unmarked as the sky's other face
And a bit of soul within the clay
    Then he spoke and the sea was born
    And I saw and marveled
And in its midst he sowed small worlds in my image and likeness
    Steeds of stone with manes erect
    and amphorae serene
    and the slanting backs of dolphins
    Ios Sériphos Síkinos Mílos
"Every word a swallow
to fetch you spring in the midst of summer," he said
And ample the olive trees
    to sift the light through their fingers
    as it spreads softly over your sleep
and so ample the cicadas
    that you do not heed them
    as you do not heed the pulse in your hand
but sparse the water
    that you may hold it a God
    and understand the meaning of its voice
and alone the tree
    without a flock of its own
    that you may take it for friend
    and know its exact name
sparse the earth beneath your feet
    that you may have nowhere to spread root
    and must reach for depth continually
and broad the sky above
    that you may read the infinite yourself

    THIS
    small, this great world!

ODYSSEUS ELÝTIS

Main village perched on thousand-foot pumice cliffs, Thira (Santorini)

Ancient harbor, Island of Sponge Divers, Kalimnos

from MYTH OF OUR HISTORY

IX

The harbor is old, I can await no longer
either the friend who left for the island of pine trees
or the friend who left for the island of plane trees
or the friend who left for the open sea.
I fondle the rusted cannon, I fondle the oars
that my body might revive and come to a decision.
The sails emit the salt smell only
of the other storm.

Since I wished to remain alone, I sought
solitude, I never sought out such an awaiting,
the fragmentation of my soul on the horizon,
these contours, these colors, this quiet.

The stars of night turn me toward the anticipation
of Odysseus for the dead among the asphodels.
When we anchored here among the asphodels we wished to find
the mountain glen that saw Adonis wounded.

GEORGE SEFÉRIS

48

Old Harbor, Island of Mykonos

Old men waiting, Piraeus Harbor

Three generations, Island of Pserimos

Waterfront town of Githion, South Peloponnesus

STONES

The days come and go without haste, without surprises.
The waters become drenched with light and memory.
One sets a stone for pillow.
Another, before swimming, leaves his clothes under a stone
so that the wind won't take them. Another keeps a stone for stool
or as a boundary mark on his farm, the cemetery, the sheepfold, the forest.

Late, after sunset, when you've returned home,
whatever stone from the seashore you placed on your table
is a statuette—a small Nike or the hound of Artemis,
and this stone, on which a young man at noon leaned his wet feet,
is a Patroclos, with shadowy, closed eyelashes.

YÁNNIS RÍTSOS

Nun cleaning rugs, old harbor below the church, Island of Kalimnos

53

Young girl's anticipation, harbor steps, Island of Samos

MARINA OF THE ROCKS

On your lips there is a taste of storm—But where have you wandered
All day long with the hard reverie of stone and sea
An eagle-bearing wind stripped the hills bare
Stripped your desire to the bone
And the pupils of your eyes seized the relay-rod of the Chimera
And lined memory with traceries of foam!
Where has it gone, the familiar slope of childhood's September

Where on red earth you played, gazing below
On the deep thickets of other girls
On corners where your friends left armfuls of rosemary

—But where have you wandered
All night long with the hard reverie of stone and sea
I would tell you to keep trace in the unclothed water of its luminous days
To lie on your back rejoicing in the dawn of all things
Or to wander again in fields of yellow
With a clover of light on your breast, O Heroine of Iambic

On your lips there is a taste of storm
And a dress crimson as blood
Deep within the summer's gold
And the hyacinth's aroma—But where have you wandered

Descending toward the shores, the pebbled bays
Where you found a cold salty seagrass
But deeper still a human emotion that bled
And opened your arms in surprise, calling its name
Lightly ascending to the limpidity of the underseas
Where your own starfish gleamed

Listen, the Word is the prudence of the aged
And Time a frenzied sculptor of men
And the sun stands above it, a beast of hope
And you, much closer, embrace a love
With a bitter taste of storm on your lips

You may no longer count on another summer, O seablue to the bone
That rivers might turn in their courses
To carry you back to their mothers
That you might kiss other cherry trees again
Or ride the horses of the Northwest Wind

Pillared on rock without yesterday or tomorrow,
On the dangers of rock, wearing the headdress of the storm
You shall say farewell to your enigma.

ODYSSEUS ELÝTIS

Storm, north coast of Cyprus

DIVER

The trap door of myth has suddenly opened again;
the ground, that seemed so solid, has abruptly subsided like a marsh,

and now you sink, a diver holding for weight
this head you had buried and that had turned to marble
in the shallow graves of oblivion.

You will find no mercy on the lips or glance
of the stone head with its hundred faces
that go on changing, uncapturable, in the depths;
and that sometimes take on the relentless visage
of repudiated selves.

Do not hope for absolution, do not await mercy
from the statues that claim life,
from the idols that do not forgive apostasy,

from the ghosts demanding justice
in the starry depths of the soul.

However artful you might have been in your negotiations,
whatever security you think you might have acquired,
they will lay ambush to your vigil and your sleep:
behind the mirrors of creation, behind Time,
you will find the stone face of reproach.

ALEXANDER MÁTSAS

Diving into ancient Greek shipwreck 16 fathoms deep, north coast of Cyprus

59

Ancient Greek shipwreck, north coast of Cyprus

Windmill on the Island of Mykonos

Secluded cove, Island of Kalimnos

THE DEATH OF ODYSSEUS

"O Water, wandering female source of life, I cup
your flux to give you a firm face and say farewell.
You warble swiftly, vanish, fluctuate and slide,
you turn all the mind's mills and all its fantasies,
nor condescend to faith, nor know what pity is.
You pierce through the black earth with rage, play with the sun,
you make the rainbows and the water-kingdoms bloom
then blot them out once more and play with other toys.
You are no peasant to strike earth's roots in my heart
but a swift-vesseled sailor who's squandered all his wealth,
glad to set sail at daybreak in a walnut shell
and leave behind all certain good, his home, his son,
virtues and feasts and comforts, all his useful gods,
and roam nude through stark foreign strands, a weathercock.
'I'm neither flesh nor mind,' you roar, 'I pass and flow
like laughter after rain, the seven-stringed sky's bow!
The mud-brained peasant lifts his startled eyes and shouts
to see my yellow, crimson or green zones foretell
his golden grain, his red wine, his green fragrant oil,
then licks his lips with greed and welcomes me with joy,
yet I'm but the rain's toy and one of the sun's smiles.
I'm not Landlady Earth, I don't sit all day long,
faithful beside my honest hearth, to await my husband,
for I sport night and day with all the sixteen winds,
and though I pluck virginity's crimson thorn-filled rose
it blossoms once again nor ever shrinks or fades.
Some call me sea, and when a ship plows through my waves,
I close its blue wake, and my honor once more blooms;
some with due reverence call me soul, an inner sea,
and deck me like a bride with breastless and dry virtues.
They call me deathless, pure, without one lump of earth,
they say I long to flee from the frail body's shame,
and though I listen to their words, I clasp flesh tight
the way a fierce girl clasps her sweetheart in the dark.
I'm not a shriveled spinster, I'm not pure, unkissed,
and I'm not chaste, nor came on earth to live a saint,
and once I clutch a body, it can't shake me off,
for never have I yearned for skies or longed for gods.

Harbor of Loutron near Khora Sfakion, Crete

Archer, I've loved you much, and now that you must go
nor leave me either your strong hands or virile thighs,
don't sigh, my tight-twined love, our time has been well spent!'"
Thus did the deep voice murmur in the archer's heart,
and when it ceased and the wave closed his bleeding wound,
the deeply bitter voice of the flesh-wrecker rang:
"O my heart's female element, O washing wave
that waters me, you draw me with you night and day,
but now we've reached that parting where embracements end."
He spoke, bent down and scooped some water in both palms
then joyed to watch it falling from his fingertips
drop by slow drop, sad, multicolored, in the sun-washed sea.

FROM THE ODYSSEY: A MODERN SEQUEL/NIKOS KAZANTZAKIS

Harbor of Khora Sfakion, Island of Crete

Young boys fishing, Island of Levkas

Whitewash, Island of Pserimos

Laundry, Island of Pserimo

ANNIVERSARY

*...even the weariest river
winds somewhere safe to sea.*

I brought my life this far
To this spot that struggles
Always near the sea
Youth on rocks, breast
To breast against the wind
Where a man may go
Who is nothing else but a man
Summing up his green moments
With coolness, the visions of his hearing
With waters, his remorses with wings
Ah, Life
Of a child who becomes a man
Always near the sea when the sun
Teaches him to breathe toward that place where
The shadow of a seagull vanishes

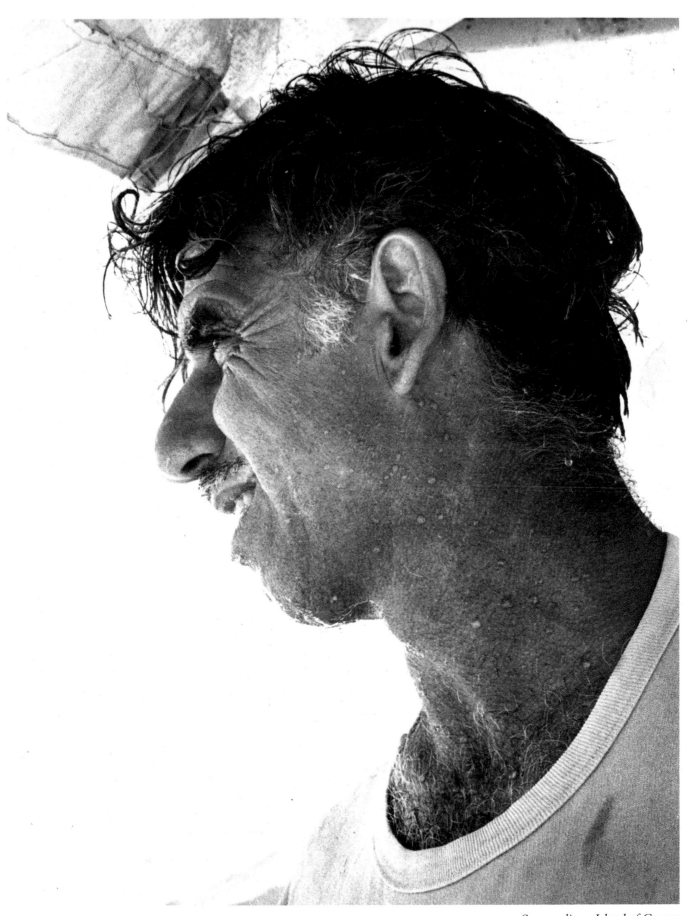

Sponge diver, Island of Cyprus

SOUTH WIND

The sea toward the west blends into a mountain range.
From our left the south wind blows and drives us mad,
this wind that strips the flesh to the bone.
Our house amid pine and carob trees.
Large windows. Large tables
to write the letters that we write you
for so many months, and we throw them
into the separation to fill it.

Star of dawn, you lowered your eyes
our hours were sweeter than oil
to the wound, more pleasing than cold water
to the plate, more soothing than feathers of the swan.
You held our life in your palm.
After the bitter bread of exile
if we remain at night before the white wall
your voice approaches us like a hope-for fire,
and again this wind hones
a razor on our nerves.

Each of us writes you the same thing
and each falls silent before the other
looking, each one, at the same world apart
at the light and the darkness upon the mountain range
and at you.

Who will lift this sorrow from our hearts?
Last night a downpour and today
the overclouded sky lowers again. Our thoughts
heaped up and useless by the door of our house
like the pine needles of yesterday's cloudburst
wish to build a tower that crumbles away.

Amid the decimation of these villages
upon this promontory exposed to the south wind
with the mountain range before us that hides you,
who will care about our decision to forget and be forgotten?
Who will accept our offering at this autumn's ending?

GEORGE SEFÉRIS

Headland, Cyprus

AGE OF BLUE MEMORY

Olive groves and vineyards as far as to the sea
Red fishing boats farther still to memory
Golden cricket husks of August in a midday sleep
With shells or seaweed. And that boat's hull
Newly built, green, that in the water's peaceful embrace still reads:
    The Lord Will Provide

Like leaves like pebbles the years went by
I remember the young men, the sailors, leaving
And painting the sails in their hearts' image
They sang of the four corners of the horizon
They wore the north winds tattooed on their chests

What was I looking for when you came painted with the sunrise
The age of the sea within your eyes
And on your body the sun's vigor—what was I looking for
Deep within sea-caverns amid spacious dreams
Where the emotions foamed of a wind
Anonymous and blue, engraving on my chest its sea emblem

With sand on my fingers, I would close my fingers
With sand in my eyes, I would clench my fingers
This was torment—
It was April, I remember, when I felt for the first time your human weight
Your human body of clay and corruption
As on our first day on earth
It was the festival of the amaryllis—But you suffered, I remember,
The wound on the bitten lip was deep
And deep the nailmark on the skin where Time is forever engraved

I left you then

And a thundering wind swept up the white houses
The white emotions freshly washed
On a sky that illumined all with a smile

Now I shall keep beside me a jug of immortal water
A form of freedom's ravaging wind
And those hands of yours where Love shall be tormented
And that shell of yours where shall echo the Aegean.

ODYSSEUS ELÝTIS

Roadside shrine to protect the Traveler, Messolongion

FIRE

Fortified houses, Mani, Southern Peloponnesus

Elder, Troodos Mountain Village, Cyprus

THE AUTOPSY

Well, it was found that the gold of the olive root had dripped into the leaves of his heart.

And because of the many times he had kept vigil close by a candle-stick, waiting for dawn to break, a strange ardor had gripped him to the marrow.

A little below the skin, the cerulean line of the horizon in a hue intense, and ample traces of azure in the blood.

It seems that the cries of birds, which in hours of great loneliness he had learned by heart, had all burst out together, so that it had not been possible for the knife to penetrate to any great depth.

Probably the intention sufficed for the Evil.

Which he confronted—it is evident—in the terrifying posture of the innocent. His eyes open and proud, the whole forest still moving on his unblemished retina.

In his brain nothing but a shattered echo of the sky.

And only in the conch of his left ear, a few grains of delicate, extremely fine sand, as in seashells. Which indicates that many times he had plodded by the sea, utterly alone, with the withering grief of love and the roar of the wind.

And as for those flakes of fire on his groin, they showed that in truth he had moved time many hours ahead whenever he had merged with a woman.

We shall have early fruit this year.

ODYSSEUS ELÝTIS

Prosperous Family, Village of Loutron, Crete

WE WALKED IN THE FIELDS ALL DAY

We walked in the fields all day
With our women our suns our dogs
We played we sang we drank water
Fresh as it sprang from the ages

In the afternoon we sat for a moment
And looked each other deeply in the eyes
A butterfly flew from our breasts
It was whiter
Than the small white branch at the tip of our dreams
We knew it was never to vanish
That it never remembered what worms it dragged along

At night we lit a fire
And around it we sang:

Fire lovely fire do not pity the logs
Fire lovely fire do not come to ash
Fire lovely fire burn us
                    tell us of life.

It is we who tell of life, we take her by the hands
We look into her eyes that look into our own
And if this that makes us drunk is a magnet, we know it
And if this that gives us pain is misfortune, we have felt it
It is we who tell of life, we go forward
And say farewell to her migrating birds

We come of a good stock.

ODYSSEUS ELÝTIS

Traditional dress, Karlavasi, Epirus

Carpenter's apprentice, Kyrenia, Cyprus

from SUMMER SOLSTICE

Now,
with the molten lead of divination
the scintillation of the summer sea,
the nakedness of life entire;
and the passing by and the stopping, the reclining and the tossing,
the lips, the fondled fleece,
all things long to burn.

So the pine tree at midday
overcome by resin
hastens to give birth to flames
and can no longer bear the torment—

call the children to gather ashes
and to sow them.
What has passed has rightly passed.
And what has not yet passed
must be burned
on this very noon when the sun was nailed
to the heart of the hundred-petaled rose.

GEORGE SEFÉRIS

Proud mother, Village of Loutron, Crete

Door, village near the Albanian border

GENEALOGY

    Where I come from they love the different fragrances
of plants and flowers
    They cut the fragrant leaves, rub them or hold them
and say, ah
    Deep is the afternoon

ELÉNI VAKALÓ

Old woman spinning, Kritsa, Crete

Stone path, Yerolimin, Mani

Grandmother's apartment, ancient harbor town of Vathi, Island of Samos

Hilltop village, Grandmother and Grandson, Republic of Cyprus

MY GRANDMOTHER'S HAT

My grandmother was a little old girl

I asked her how she had fallen in love the very first time

    I wore a hat

    At the end of the branch a nest
    Rested on my neck
    And there were birds there too

    The birds flew

ELÉNI VAKALÓ

Greek family, Island of Levkas

BEHIND EVERY DOOR

There is a land composed of song
There are promises made for our voices
Nor by death nor by daydreams
Beloved hands as they touch our foreheads
Glances that move within us like birds in the sky
Leaving behind them the tremor of a present happiness

If tomorrow you find me speechless
Deprived even of a tree's shade
The previous time would have borne fruit on my skin
You would have approached me and then left, remembering me

This is why you have heard my step on every stair,
And behind every door
I stand and knock.

D.P. PAPADHÍTSAS, in *The Charioteer*

High mountain village near the Albania border

Widow, small village, Mani

from AXION ESTI

PSALM XVIII

Now I'm marching on to a distant and unwrinkled land.
Now azure girls follow me
    and stone ponies
with the sun's wheel on their wide brows.
    Generations of myrtles recognize me
from that the time when I trembled on the iconostasis of water,
    crying out to me, holy, holy.
He that defeated Hell, he that liberated Love
    he is the Prince of Lilies.
And for a moment I was once more painted
    by those same zephyrs of Crete,
that crocus yellow might receive justice from the empyrean.
    Now in whitewash I enclose and entrust
my true Laws.
    Blessed, I say, are the strong who decode the Immaculate,
for their teeth alone is the grape–nipple that intoxicates
    on the breasts of volcanoes and the vineshoots of virgins.
Behold, let them follow in my footsteps!
    Now I'm marching on to a distant and unwrinkled land.
Now it is the hand of Death
    that bestows Life,
and sleep does not exist.
    The churchbells of midday are ringing
and slowly on sunhot rocks are engraved these words:
    NOW and AYE and WORTHY IT IS
Aye aye and now now warble the birds.
    WORTHY is the price paid.

ODYSSEUS ELÝTIS

Merchant, Yerolimin, Mani

Young Girl, beach of Pserimos

from BODY OF SUMMER

"O naked body of summer, burnt
And eaten away by oil and salt
Body of rock and the heart's tremor
Great fluttering in the willow's hair
Breath of basil on the curly groin
Filled with starlets and pine needles
Profound body, vessel of day!"

The slow rains come, the pelting hail,
The shores pass by, flogged by the claws of the wintry wind
That with savage billows slowes in the sea–depths
The hills plunge into thick cloud udders
But behind all this you smile unconcernedly
And find again your deathless hour
As once more you are found on the beaches by the sun
And amid your naked vigor by the sky.

ODYSSEUS ELÝTIS

ODYSSEUS BLESSES HIS LIFE

May you be blessed, my life, that passed the heaviest trial
of all, and with the light breath of a spring's cool breeze
knocked down the fortress of my own unpitying ego.
Then slowly as I grew more gentle, I longed to pass
even beyond sweet large–eyed Love and in my arms
clasp tight all of my native land like a maid's body.
O glittering harbors, sand–smooth beaches, tossing boats,
mountains with crystal waters and the pungent thyme,
old crones who spin their wool, maidens with fertile wombs,
brave gallant lads who fight the earth or foaming sea,
stones, bodies, souls, how could my mind contain you all?

NÍKOS KAZANTZÁKIS
From *The Odyssey: A Modern Sequel*, XVI

Old shepherd, Loutron, Crete

A STROLL IN THE PRESENT

Amorous games
kisses and kisses
breasts of girls and women
lilies and roses

My memory feels a caress
I bathe my eyes
I leave my hands
in the clearest water

I climb an azure mountain
(and look at the sea)
that keeps watching me)
I reach the summit
an unexpected sky
And I confront the clouds

and between the clouds my years
intact

GEORGE SARANDÁRIS

Village farmer, Loutron, Crete

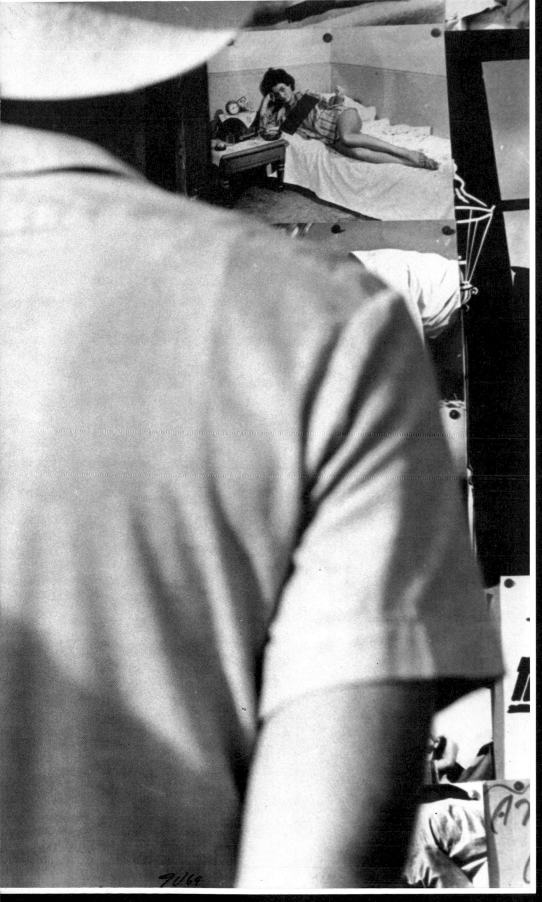

AIR

Movie billboard, modern city of Megalopolis, Peloponesus

THE MEANING OF SIMPLICITY

I hide behind simple things that you may find me;
if you don't find me, you'll find the things,
you'll touch what my hand touches,
the imprints of our hands will merge.

The August moon glitters in the kitchen
like a pewter pot (it becomes like this because of what I tell you)
it lights up the empty house and the kneeling silence of the house—
always the silence remains kneeling.

Every word is a way out
for an encounter often canceled,
and it's then a word is true, when it insists on the encounter.

YÁNNIS RÍTSOS

Children off to school, Megalopolis

Harbor tavern, Kyrenia, Cyprus

Knife maker, Monasteraki section, Athens

112

Lottery and corn seller, Monasteraki, Athens

Basket seller, Omonia Square, Athens

Visitor and Zeus, National Museum of Archaeology, Athens

The Philosophers, National Museum of Archaeology, Athens

THE STATUES

During the day even the statues have no expression.
If as it sometimes happens in a movie theater
the projecting machine should suddenly stop,
though the electric fan still keeps on running,
you will notice that on every fixed face immobility wears
an arrested mask caught in a frozen expression.
During the day statues wear a similar kind of mask.

But when night slowly begins to emerge from the thick
foliage, to creep softly with circumspection
and then stand with closed eyelids behind the back
of the park keeper, he shudders without knowing why.

He notices the hour, seizes the bell's tongue suddenly
and breaks open its enclosures of sound to the startled air.
Then the birds become small marble figures,
and the last cries of children hang frozen in mid-air.

Night binds time tightly to the locked iron gate.
But how can the statues feel time's crucifixion
since they hang about it, hovering in mid-air?
They seem to be like those stopped alarm clocks
that have lost their ancient, primordial memory.
Night winds them up one by one, and then withdraws.

Now the statues remember, feel the swarming itch
of time, and their naked bodies shiver.
Then they wear their masks inside out
and step down from their pedestals to stretch awhile.

But now they are not what they presented
to petrified time. This girl who cups
her naked breasts, like a white bird,
is not a girl. She is the spirit which has shaped her
and dwelt in her from the beginning. Now
she remembers, shivers, and falls in love with herself.

During the day the statues have no future. The museums,
into which they sometimes withdraw with weariness,
are the lost cemeteries of the past
wherein death holds time in a narcotic trance.

The statues possess only the past: but not that
eternally present in the marble quarries.
This is that decisive moment of the past when the spirit
has come to dwell in them forever.
But as soon as it became present, the alarm clock stopped
and cast away its key into the vast night.
And on their white faces time turned immovably to stone.

Night now holds their key; she winds them up
one by one, then transports them into the future
that stretches out beyond time: because night
is beyond time and beyond death.

G. T. VAFÓPOULOS

116

"Mask of Agamemnon", National Museum of Archaeology, Athens

Group of Aphrodite, Pan and Eros from Delos, being studied by visitor, National Museum of Archaeology, Athens

Past beckons, National Museum of Archaeology, Athens

Present time, Kolonaki Square, Athens

THE FRONTIER

In order to pass through this frontier, you must
strip yourself of all memories; you must leave
fear on the threshold; you must lay down your love.
The saints, you see, travel without luggage,
stripped of harvests reaped by all their senses.

But as they pass, they pause a moment, turn their faces
back, as though remembering something: far it seems
they have forgotten to take off all their clothing.
They cast all off and then proceed: for beyond time,
far beyond silence, far beyond all solitude.

That forest you sense is not composed of trees.
It is made of rocks that have assumed the new
bodies of saints in which their spirits dwell.
They do not move, they do not speak, they do not feel.
For they communicate through underground
deep passages, and this is the reason why
they understand each other only.

These birds you see killed, as though they had fallen
with violence and struck the frontier wall,
are not birds: they are the small, empty bodies
they have discarded, for they had no other clothes.
The birds are now far, far away; they stand on those rocks,
but you cannot see them, cannot hear them, you cannot even feel them.
Yet they exist: far beyond love, far beyond time,
far beyond silence, far beyond all solitude.

You cannot pass over while you wear these clothes.
How can you take them off now, for they have grown on you!
And if you try to strip them off, you will remain
entirely within them; nothing will then be left
of what you were or shall be, that may pass over.

You are a foliage filled with memories; a chord
stretched taut between the children and the saints
that time has built with tree-rings round and round
like the slow growth of a primordial tree.
But how can you become a rock, for although
it understands, it does not feel. Your throbbing chord,
although built in, is still shot through with senses.

You are a tree. And thus you know that trees
do not travel; they only feel, and remember.

G. T. VAFÓPOULOS

Merchant, Vathi, Samos

LACONIC

Ardor for death so inflamed me that my radiance returned to the sun,
And it sends me back into the perfect syntax of stone and air.
Well then, he whom I sought *I am*.
O flaxen summer, prudent autumn,
Slightest winter,
Life pays the obol of an olive leaf
And in a night of fools once again confirms with a small cricket
     the lawfulness of the Unhoped-For.

ODYSSEUS ELÝTIS

Village Papas, Mani, southern Peloponnesus

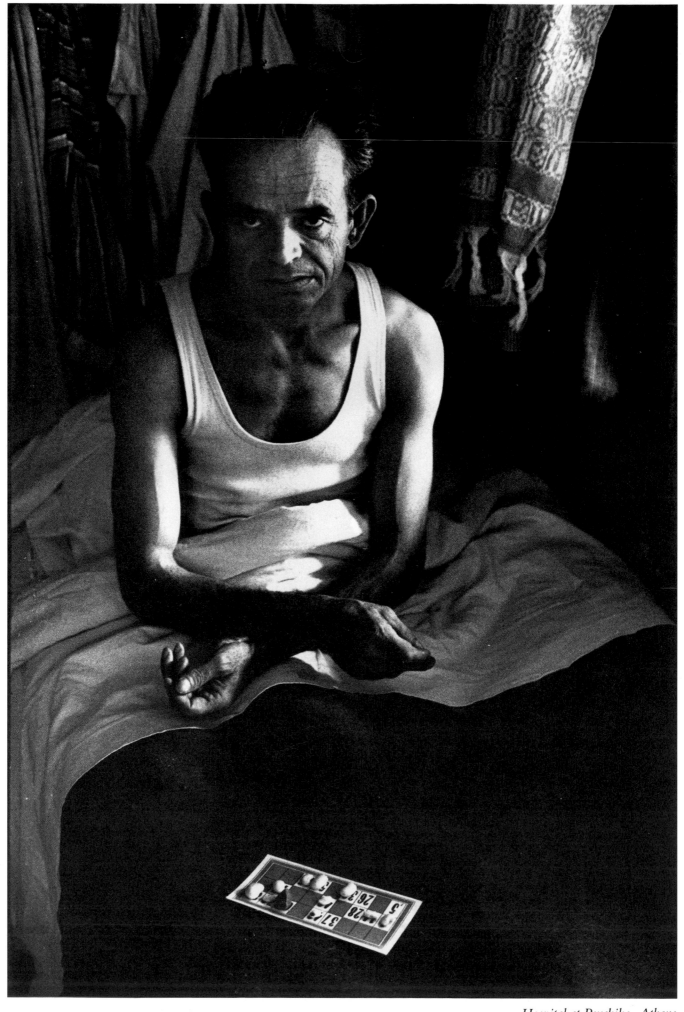

Hospital at Psychiko, Athens

Pantokrator, Andiphonodis, Cyprus

Hospital at Psychiko, Athens

PSYCHE'S ADVENTURE

While her beautiful vestments decline
with the rich ecstasy of the flesh,
the Soul pursues tirelessly her great adventure,
hidden behind a thousand illusions,

hidden behind hours, days, years,
    hidden behind yourself.

Like the gleaner who timidly follows the harvesters,
she gathers much that on your way you despised,
behind actions, behind words, behind thoughts,
    behind labor and sleep.

With these fragments she shapes the powerful figures
that rule the inexorable firmament of Myth,
always uncapturable, but ever so close
that you feel their breathing and their command
    behind the scenery.

Thus you may sometimes recapture the outcast
Soul, in some abyss of silence or some tear;
when the body unexpectedly shivers under a breath
    of life, from the lips of death.

ALEXANDER MÁTSAS

Interior of Bus, old shepherd crossing the White Mountains of Crete

Traditional dress, Kyrenia, Cyprus

from AXION ESTI

PROPHETIC VI

Holy relics of old stars and cobwebbed corners of the sky swept by the storm to be born out of the mind of man. But before this, lo, generations will guide their ploughs over the barren earth. And the Governors will secretly count their human merchandise, declaring wars. Whereupon the Policeman and the Military Judge will be sated, leaving gold to the insignificant that they may themselves collect the wages of insult and martyrdom. And large ships will hoist flags, martial music will take to the streets, balconies will shower the Victor with flowers—who shall be living in the stench of corpses. And next to him, unfolding to his measure, darkness will gape open like a pit, crying: Exiled Poet, speak, what do you see in your century?

—I see Military Judges burning like candles on the great table of the
  Resurrection.

—I see Policemen offering their blood as sacrifice to the purity of the skies.

—I see the unending revolution of plants and flowers.

—I see the gunboats of Love's powers.

ODYSSEUS ELÝTIS

Greek Navy guard, Kyrenia, Cyprus

133

Three workmen, Megalopolis, central Peloponnesus

Steps, Island of Mykonos

BUILDERS

Have you seen those who build out of instinct
and those who build professionally
and the third who build to revenge themselves against death
and those who build consciously, with resolution?

Both these and the others stop from time to time,
wipe their plastered hands on their blue jeans,
wipe away their sweat, and weep.
They do not wipe their eyes.

In this way, moreover, the mortar knits better.
And this proceeds much *beyond* their purpose.
Because of this, all the builders dream at night
of that unknown, that invisible "beyond,"
and every morning they build the "here" a bit better.

YÁNNIS RÍTSOS

135

Children of different cultures, old town, Rhodes

GLITTERING DAY, CONCH OF THE VOICE

Glittering day, conch of the voice that created me
Naked, to walk on my daily Sundays
Amid the welcoming cry of seashores
Blow on the first-known wind
Spread out an affectionate green meadow
On which the sun may roll his head
And light up poppies with his lips
Poppies that proud men will pluck
So there may be no other mark on their naked chests
Than the blood of carefree disdain that erased sorrow
Reaching as far as the memory of freedom

I spoke of love, of the rose's health, the sunray
That alone finds the heart straightway
Of Greece that walks the sea with surety
Of Greece that takes me on voyages always
To naked snow-glorious mountains

I give my hand to justice
Translucent fountain, spring on the mountain summit
My sky is deep and unchanging
Whatever I love is born unceasingly
Whatever I love is always at its beginning.

ODYSSEUS ELÝTIS

Grape harvest on the hills above Rethimnon, Crete

A Reawakening—The Poetry of Modern Greece

Greece has been a free modern nation for only a little over 140 years. During the almost 400 years of the Turkish occupation, her language and culture were suppressed while other European nations were flourishing in their renaissances. Ever since regaining her liberty, Greece has weathered two world wars, two Balkan wars, several military coups and civil wars. It is only in recent times that her culture in the arts, after long slumber, has begun to bloom. I am in complete agreement with Professor Constantine A. Trypanis, former Minister of the Sciences and the Arts, when he refers to Greek poetry as that "with the longest and perhaps noblest tradition in the Western world," and who concludes that "in the last hundred years greater and more original poetry has been written in Greek than in the fourteen centuries which preceded them," and that "in the last fifty years it has at last achieved universal validity." From my own reading in European and world poetry, I would say that modern Greek poetry is as fine as any written anywhere today. It is no small tribute that such a small country should have, in the small space of only sixteen years, been twice granted the Nobel Prize in Poetry, and that it has had recently, and still has, other poets equally worthy of the honor.

For centuries unaffected by the distracting currents of a swiftly changing world beyond their boundaries, the Greek shepherds herded their sheep amid the Cyclopean walls of Tiryns and Mycenae (worn to a smooth polish by the brushing of sheeps' wool); the Greek farmers casually placed on their mantles bits of pottery and fragments of statues they had plowed up in their fields, or embedded into the walls of their humble huts classical torsos or Byzantine inscriptions; the Greek fishermen, amid dolphins that once carried poets on their backs, caught in their nets fishes that peddlers in the streets of Piraeus hawked with their ancient and hallowed names. Although the common people of Greece had long lost almost all of their intellectual and conscious connections with the past, they sank deeper into their ancestral soil, sea and language, and in their isolation were subconsciously infused and pervaded by voices, roots, traditions, rituals, songs and ceremonies which had become the substance and essence of their blood and bones. They could not define or explain the relevance or significance of their emotions or their acts, but in dancing, singing, speaking, building, or in their almost mystical identification with rock, sea and sky, there *were* what they could not analyze. The Greek poet, conscious of the fructifying nature of such demotic sources, makes periodic visits to his rural birthplace or ancestral village to keep in touch with the ground roots of his common heritage.

I have always thought that a poem cannot be directly illustrated. Any attempt at forthright reproduction of aural and visional imagery in visual terms cannot but disappoint expectations in the minds of disparate readers with disparate interpretations of the poem; worse, it can, by offering a concrete, specific image, limit or deaden the imagination or interpretation. On the other hand, if no attempt is made at direct illustration or analogy, poem and photograph (or painting), when juxtaposed, can borrow imagery and meaning from each other, extend peripheries of each other's suggestions, and create a rainbow bridge of aural, orchestral, visual and visionary strands that enrich one another and yet still retain individuality. Although the poems I have chosen for John Veltri's photographs are not meant, therefore, to label or define them, both have, nevertheless, distinct points of reference; enough, I hope, to excite in the imagination of viewer and reader a sensual and mental enrichment. Each poem and each photograph should retain a first its own special identity, but then gradually merge to some degree into the mind and senses in order to excite an aesthetic experience that would have been depleted had either poem or photograph been read or viewed separately. It is my hope that the integrity of the book as a whole may reveal, or an intermingled plane of aesthetic imagery, the extraordinarily multifaceted grace and strength of the Greek people and their landscape.

KIMON FRIAR

POETS BIOGRAPHIES

ODYSSEUS ELÝTIS

Odysseus Elýtis was born in Iráklion, Crete, in 1911 but has lived in Athens since 1914, spending his summers in the Aegean islands and traveling extensively in Europe and in the United States. He studied literature at the Sorbonne (University of Paris, France), associating closely with the poets and painters of the Parisian School and writing art critiques for Greek and French periodicals. He has held many administrative positions in Greece in theater, radio, and ballet organizations. He was awarded by Greece the First State Prize in Poetry, by the University of Thessaloníki and the University of London honorary degrees, and in 1979 the Nobel Prize in Literature. Elýtis has written that Kimon Friar's translations of his selected poems, *The Sovereign Sun*, was significant in his being awarded the Nobel Prize.

NÍKOS KAZANTZÁKIS

Níkos Kazantzákis was born In Iráklion, Crete, in 1883 and died in a hospital clinic in Freiburg, Germany, in 1957. He studied at the University of Athens and at the Sorbonne (University of Paris, France), then traveled in many parts of the world, writing travel books on many countries. He has translated about fifty books, including the epics of Homer, Dante, and Goethe, and has written his own epic, *The Odyssey: A Modern Sequel*, which has been translated into English iambic hexameter by Kimon Friar. Kazantzákis has written many novels, plays and film scenarios, an autobiography, philosophical studies and essays. He was awarded the International Peace Prize in 1957, and has been nominated several times for the Nobel Prize.

ALEXANDER MÁTSAS

Alexander Mátsas was born in Athens in 1910 and died in London in 1969. He studied in Greece at the University of Athens and in Great Britain at Oxford University, then joined the Greek Diplomatic Service. He represented his country in Egypt, France, Belgium, Italy, Turkey, Pakistan, and was Ambassador to the United States in 1962-67. In addition to poetry, he has written poetic drama.

D. P. PAPADHÍTSAS

Dhimítrios Papadhítsas was born on Sámos in 1922. He received the degree in medicine from the University of Athens in 1942, then served as orthopedic surgeon in several hospitals in Athens and Sparta and conducted a private clinic in Kalamáta. He has represented Greece in many international poetry symposiums in Europe, and won the First State Prize in poetry in 1963.

YÁNNIS RÍTSOS

Yánnis Rítsos was born in the Peloponnesos in 1909. For his left-wing activities, he has been incarcerated in various detention camps several times over many years. He has published close to a hundred books of poetry and translation and has received honors and awards from almost every European country. He has been nominated ten times for the Nobel Prize in Literature.

GEORGE SARANDÁRIS

George Sarandáris was born on April 14, 1907 in Istanbul but lived with his family in Italy until the age of twenty-four. He came to Greece in 1931 for military service, made infrequent trips to Italy, and died on February 26, 1941 from war related injuries. A person of restless intellectual curiosity, articulate, critical, changing from idea to idea, rich in philosophical nuance, contemptuous of the hedonist and the materialist, he sought for the essence of things, impatient with forms and artifice and wrote with clarity and point.

GEORGE SEFÉRIS

George Seféris was born in Smyrna, Turkey, in 1900 and died in Athens in 1971. After studies in Athens and Paris, he joined the Greek Diplomatic Service and served his country in many posts, last as Ambassador to Great Britain in 1957-62. He was granted honorary degrees by the universities of Cambridge, Oxford, Princeton, and Thessaloníki, was elected an Honorary Member of the American Academy of Arts and Sciences, and was awarded the Foyle Prize in Poetry, London, 1962, and the Nobel Prize in Literature in 1963.

GEORGE THÉMELIS

George Thémelis was born on the island of Samos in 1900 and died in Thessaloníki in 1976. He earned the degree in literature from the University of Thessaloníki and taught Greek language and literature in various high schools, particularly in the Experimental School at the University of Thessaloníki 1934-49. In addition to his poetry, he has translated ancient Greek plays, published several scholarly works (particularly on Greek language and literature), and written three important books on literary criticism of his fellow poets and Greek poetry in general. He was awarded the First State Prize in Poetry for 1961.

G. T. VAFÓPOULOS

G. T. Vafópoulos was born in 1903 in what was then Turkey and is now part of Yugoslavia. At the outbreak of the First World War his family moved to Thessaloníki, where he has lived ever since, primarily as Director of the Municipal Library there. He has traveled extensively in Europe and the United States. He was given the First State Prize for 1966 and the Oúranis Award of the Athens Academy in 1971, and was made a Corresponding Member of the Athens Academy in 1980.

ELÉNI VAKALÓ

Eléni Vakaló was born in Athens in 1921, took her degree in archeology at the University of Athens, and studied the history of art at the Sorbonne (University of Paris), France. In collaboration with her husband and others she founded the Vakaló School of Decorative Arts in 1958. She teaches the history of art and has become one of the foremost art critics in Greece. In 1965 she toured the United States and in 1967 took part in the Harvard International Seminar. In addition to her poetry, she has written many books on art.

"This is my music, in your photographs!"

MIKIS THEODORAKIS